MW00577028

WALK WITH ME

An Invitation to Faith

NEAL B. FREEMAN

Walk with Me: An Invitation to Faith

© 2021 by Neal B. Freeman

For information contact
National Review Books
19 West 44th Street
New York, NY 10036

Cover design by Luba Myts

Names: Freeman, Neal B., author.
Title: Walk with me : an invitation to faith / Neal
B. Freeman.
Description: New York, NY : National Review
Books, [2021] |
Identifiers: ISBN: 978-0-9847650-6-5
Subjects: LCSH: Freeman, Neal B. | Conversion. |
Religion. | Faith. | Protestantism. | Prayer. | Spiritu-
ality. | Spiritual life. | LCGFT: Essays.
Classification: LCC: BL639 .F74 2021 | DDC:
204/.2092—dc23

PRINTED IN THE UNITED STATES OF AMERICA

This book is dedicated to
Miss Jane Louise Metze Freeman
for her outstanding performance
in a leading role.

TABLE OF CONTENTS

FROM THE BEGINNING

I love those stories of religious conversion. Everybody does, I suppose. Those journeys of faith, as they've come to be called, have what we all need in the way of a brow-smoothing and heart-lifting tale. We are asked, first, to commiserate. We wade into the slop waters of a wasting life. There, we encounter dysfunction, abuse, and self-diminishment of one sort or another. In this opening sequence, the possibilities for purposeless life are omnipresent—and seemingly unavoidable.

Then, in the search for some transcendent meaning to human existence, we are tugged along through the mean streets of a dystopian world. The path is steep and poorly lit.

Finally, with both writer and reader at nerve's end, we hear the peal of heavenly thunder. Praise be! He has arrived! In this closing scene, with the journey at last completed, our seeker of faith falls into the loving arms of a forgiving God.

Those are fine stories, inspiring stories, but yours is not likely to find a place among them. It is even less likely that your story will bear any resemblance to the paradigmatic conversion story.

****

Born about the same time as Jesus, Paul became,

against all odds, the second most important person in the history of the world's most widely practiced religion.* He was not the obvious choice for his earth-changing role. Paul was a Pharisee, after all. He was a Roman citizen. He was the loyal son of a devoutly religious family, who performed his filial duty with vigor—by persecuting Christians.

Paul was a good Jewish boy, that is, until the day he wasn't. Sometime around 30 A.D., Paul set out from Jerusalem on the dusty road to Damascus. It was a business trip, basically. Paul's tools as a tentmaker were portable and his potential customer base thus stretched from one horizon to the other. Across Asia Minor, as it was once called, everybody could use a good tent.

After some depleting days on the parched road, Paul was stunned by an apparition. Jesus Christ, the risen Lord Himself, appeared to Paul in a vision. A blinding vision. Only with the help of his traveling companions was Paul able to find his way into the city. It took three days to recover his eyesight. And only then did he come to appreciate that his life had been changed radically, and for the rest of his life. Paul had received, directly from the lips of Jesus, the timeless Word of God. Paul heard it, he accepted it, and he resolved to preach it *urbe et orbe.* It was a simple message of great power. It went like this: God had sent his only Son to save us earthbound sinners. The

* Some observers would reserve that distinction for Peter, but his role seems more titular, Paul's more operational. We can argue the point another time.

Son had been crucified—murdered!—not for His sins but for ours. The Son had then risen to be with his Father, but He would come again soon. And, most reverberatingly of all, there was this final assurance from Jesus to Paul: The sinners who believed in the Son would live with Him forever.

The judgment of history, manifestly, has been that Paul's message was more powerful than simple. Down through the years it has turned millions of people from their own empty lives to new and full lives in Christ: Paul's has been a message of great spiritual force. Almost from the beginning, though, it has been a message that both confused lay readers and entangled Biblical scholars. Almost from the beginning, there have been questions, nagging questions.

One of the first and most persistent of those questions was about Paul's use of the word "soon." What, precisely, was the meaning of that word? *Sub specie aeternitatis,* as Paul might have put it during his Latin phase, the 2,000 years we sinners have just spent sinning could be interpreted as no more than the blink of an eye. Our Lord will come again, that is to say, but we should not expect to see Him next Thursday. The trouble here is that for most of us plainspoken and impatient folk, "soon" would seem to suggest a matter of weeks or months rather than of millennia. So, was Paul wrong or, worse, misleading about this essential detail? Has his message been discredited by the passage of time? A nagging question, that.

Or take Paul's final promise, the assurance that sinners who believed in Jesus would be rewarded with eternal life. As Paul explains it in his letters to emerging Christian communities, salvation is achieved neither by exertions of human reason nor by the good works of lives well lived. According to Paul, salvation is a gift from God to his flawed children—an outright and unconditional gift. That seems clear enough, but then there is this passage from Paul: "May your spirit and soul and body be kept sound and blameless at the coming of our Lord Jesus Christ." What are we to make of that? Has Paul just slapped a draconian condition on what had appeared to be an unfettered benefaction? Maybe not. Paul's injunction may be more velleity than stricture. My own reading, which would be cringe-worthy in scholarly circles, is that Paul was simply recycling a trope from his youth, when a favorite uncle might have said with a touch of the tummler, *Live a good life? Hey, Paulie, it couldn't hurt.*

These are just two of the many questions, all of them vexing, that Paul labored to answer over the course of his long evangelical career. (Well, ask yourself: Wouldn't you have a question or two if a stranger offered you eternal life with no strings attached?) Paul's answers, artfully calibrated and beautifully crafted, are set out in his letters to the early Christian enclaves—the Corinthians, the Galatians, and the rest. Of the 27 books in the New Testament, 13 or 14 are attributed with varying degrees of confidence to Paul. At least seven of the books, scholars seem to have agreed, are almost certainly from Paul himself. (A 15th book, Acts, or in some versions Acts of the Apostles, is in large part *about* Paul and his prodigious good works.) Taken together as a kind of instruction manual for those new to the faith, Paul's words told the world for the first time what it means to be a Christian.

Take his Letter to the Romans, his best and final letter. It is generally regarded, along with the Gospels of Matthew and John, as one of the most influential texts in all of Christian scripture. For centuries, prominent faith leaders have given credit for their own inspiration to the "Pauline gospel" as Paul had limned it in Romans, including such disparate figures as Saint Augustine, John Calvin, and Martin Luther King Jr. The byline on the New Testament, had it ever carried one, might properly have been, *Jesus as told to Paul.*

If Paul's message turned out to be not all that simple, then, there has been no gainsaying its power. The guesstimates currently available tell us that there are three truly global religions in the early part of the 21st century. There are 1.2 billion Hindus, 1.9 billion Muslims, and 2.3 billion Christians. That's a lot of conversions. And that's the triumphantly good news of the Gospel according to Paul.

As we've come to learn, though, there's nothing easy about Paul the Apostle. There's some not-so-good news here, too. The evidence compiled to this point in Christian history is clear on the salient point: When it comes to your own hopes for conversion, you will in all likelihood *not* have a Pauline experience. The risen Christ will *not* appear to you in a blinding vision. He will *not* personally deliver unto you the distilled wisdom of Heaven. And you will *not* be converted instantaneously from whatever incumbent beliefs you currently hold to a gloriously new (and occasionally confusing) faith called Christianity.

No, it is much more likely that you will have to make your own way toward faith. And, because you are oh-so human and not-at-all divine, you will proceed with neither a sure pace nor a set purpose. No, you will zig and zag. You will wander and falter. You will fall short, miss the mark, stub your toe, and trip over a shoelace. You will frustrate your shepherds, embarrass your loved ones, and, on more than a few occasions, mortify yourself. You will approach your destination not with straight-line resolve but, rather, asymptotically, always coming closer but never quite arriving at a perfect faith.

Until the day, of course, that you do—until the day that you join the company of those 2.3 billion other human beings who have shuffled on before you, those deeply flawed human beings whose stumblings offer constant hope that you can overcome your own travail. You can't help but notice that, even with all of their overstuffed, won't-fit-into-the-overhead-compartment baggage, those blessed stumblebums managed to make it all the way home. You can, too, you tell yourself, and not unreasonably.

You've heard that tired saying, "Even the longest journey begins with a single step." Don't take it literally. It is one of the most misleading sentences in the English language. Why? Because of the embedded implication that each step is somehow commensurate with every other step—the implication that your journey is just a series of measured strides, one after the other, with no single step falling any longer or shorter than any other. Now, that may be true if you're hiking the upland trails or fetching a quart of milk or giving the dog a chance to stretch his legs. But if you're seeking God—if you are embarked on an all-in, no-kidding journey of faith—it's not true at all.

When you're walking toward God, there are no easy steps. Happily, the last step is short, clearly demarked and, by that point in your journey, attained with little effort. We all know how warm and welcoming it feels to plant a road-worn shoe on a familiar front porch.

And from hard-won, lab-tested experience we know that the steps along the way are many and tentative, some of them misdirected, some of them doubling back on each other. We know the general direction in which we should be headed, but the exact route is beyond our ken and known only to Him. But even the most debauched among us can put one foot in front of the other.

There is one step that is different from all the others. By taking it, we announce our willingness to leave behind our old selves. We agree to open the door to the certain perils and uncertain rewards of a new life. By taking that first step, we commit ourselves to completing our journey of faith, or to die trying.

The purpose of this book is to invite you to take that first step. Please, walk with me.

WHITE, ANGLO, SAXON, AND ALMOST PROTESTANT

One of the most heuristic things ever said about a member of my family was said by William Bradford, governor of Plymouth colony, the early American settlement located in what would, at a later day, become the Commonwealth of Massachusetts. Writing in his memoir, *Of Plymouth Plantation*, Bradford said of my paternal ancestor, William Brewster, "He was tenderhearted and compassionate of such as were in misery but especially of such as had been of good estate and rank and were fallen unto want and poverty. . . ." What was remarkable in that encomium, of course, was not the contention that Brewster was a nice man. Down through the centuries, the record would probably confirm that my family has produced at least one nice man every generation or so. What was remarkable was that Brewster was revered not so much for his work in comforting the afflicted as for his success in comforting the formerly comfortable. As the Elder—the spiritual leader, that is to say—of a small band of English Christians who decamped first to Leiden, Holland, and then to America in 1620 on the good ship *Mayflower*, Brewster was tending to a relatively well-placed and well-connected flock. These were merchants and farmers, men of the law, men of the Book.

These Pilgrims, as they came to be called, were not

low-born or criminal elements fleeing authority in search
of a second chance. (For the footloose and felonious, con-
veniently, there would soon be Australia.) These were
proper Englishmen, some of them educated, which was
rare in those days, and most of them with "good
prospects." What set them apart from the rest of their
countrymen was a determination to worship God according to their own lights, free from constraints imposed by
the mighty Church of England, and free as well from an
English king increasingly given to what the Pilgrims per-
ceived to be papist tendencies. These Pilgrims were men
and women willing and, in notable cases, eager to subor-
dinate the temporal to the transcendent. They were, as history would later inscribe, the brave souls who brought
across a vast ocean and then planted in the hard soil of
New England the radical and very American idea of religious freedom. That idea took root, deep root. Almost two
centuries later, the constitutional Framers would begin the
very first sentence of the very first clause of the Bill of
Rights this way: "Congress shall make no law respecting
an establishment of religion, or prohibiting the free exercise thereof."

Another way of looking at that hardy congregation
huddled aboard the *Mayflower*, of course, is to say that
they were a boatload of religious fanatics, led in matters
religious by the most fanatical congregant among them—
my man Brewster.

My mother's family arrived somewhat later. She was
a descendant of John Winthrop, who arrived in New Eng-

land aboard the *Arbella* in 1630. He settled on the shores
of Massachusetts Bay and, as a dogged and competitive
sort, busied himself with the task of building a community
superior to Plymouth, which was situated just a few miles
down the Atlantic coast. Winthrop was a drumbeater. He
is perhaps best known to history for urging his fellow
colonists to appreciate that the eyes of the world were
upon them and that, accordingly, they should "consider
that we shall be as a City upon a Hill"—that is, that they
should conduct themselves so as to serve as shining examples for those left behind in Old England. (Notable political figures, Ronald Reagan prominent among them,
would consider Winthrop's exhortation to be the *fons et
origo* of the worldview known today as "American ex-
ceptionalism.")

Winthrop was a man of this world and less so of the
next. He was, in the contemporary formulation, a community organizer: The trains, had they yet been invented,
would surely have run on time. In matters of the spirit he
made even Brewster look like a theological wimp.
Winthrop looked with undisguised disdain on the loose,
disorganized ways of Plymouth. His own Puritans were,
in his estimate at least, much improved versions of Brewster's Pilgrims. In return, the Pilgrims set the pattern for
the next 400 years of American immigration by looking
askance at the bumptious Puritans who "came later." (To
the 21st-century eye, it should be conceded, the distinction
between the two groups seems without much difference.)

Winthrop had a taste for rhetorical combat and a wont

for doctrinal scab-picking. In one such occasion, he incited a canonical fight of obscure origin with a young woman who lived just across the street, a firebrand named Anne Hutchinson. She and her band of followers, all of whom—in Winthrop's unsparing view—had wandered from the true Christian path, were ultimately driven from the Massachusetts Bay colony into the wilds of Rhode Island, where Hutchinson became a major colonial figure in her own right. The true path for most New Englanders in those formative years was pretty much what John Winthrop said it was. (I should note for the record that I find my distant cousin John Winthrop, who is entitled but has so far declined to affix the Roman numeral XI to his surname, to be not in the least bit censorious. It is widely believed, in fact, that he is the nice man in my own generation.)

Brewster and Winthrop—my men, my founding fathers.

We have by this point established that the writer of these words is, roughly speaking, the WASPiest man in America. Verily, I have been bred within an inch of my life and could be installed neither painted nor powdered as a free-standing exhibit in the Peabody Museum. Curators there might extract a princely sum from tourists seeking selfies with the one-and-only, WASP Man.

But does this unusual genetic inheritance mean anything special? Does it mean that I was born on third base? Does it mean that as I make my way in life, ornate and filigreed doors swing open at my approach? Does it mean, for specific instance, that I will be invited to join the law firm of Cadwallader, Wickersham & Taft? (Just kidding. I like the sound of the place. The only name missing from the letterhead is that of my favorite Wodehouse character, Galahad Threepwood. For all I know, the firm may be run these days by three young women named Petrillo, Gold-farb, and Ulasciewisz.) Does it mean that I will be invited to join a snooty club such as, say, The Knickerbocker? (The last time I was there it smelled like my grand-mother's house. You know, *that* smell.) Does it mean that I will be surrounded by rich girls? (It actually did mean that in my ill-spent youth. But as I was not the first to learn, rich girls tend to be pinched in their affections and guilt-stricken in their politics. Having fun with a rich girl can be hard work.)

Skipping to the bottom line, does the WASP inheri-tance include—you'll excuse the expression—money? Does the bloodline carry with it downstream both a trust fund and the cossetting of family office? I'm glad you asked. The answer, at the tail end of a long line of desic-cated WASPs, is almost always: Uh, not really.

In my own case, the family tree is festooned with the names of the well-born, the (occasionally) well-meaning and, here and there, the well-known. (A Ralph W. Emer-son is recorded there, at the end of one twisty branch.) But men of affairs? Men of deed and daring? Men who, to be frank, did anything useful? Or made anything use-ful? Candles? Canoe paddles? Woolen socks? Uh, not re-ally. There were preachers, lots of preachers—the Mather boys, Increase (once-president of Harvard, of course) and

Cotton, Jonathan Edwards, and a century-long skein of Moodys who pounded the pulpit to smithereens at the old First Parish Church in York, Maine. Many members of my attenuated tribe, in truth, could have used some of Brewster's anodyne touch, and especially those several kinfolk who "had been of good estate and rank and were fallen unto want."

Happily, I had no such problem myself. While I was privileged to move in uptown circles and to attend elite schools, I knew from an early age that, socially advantaged as I was, there would be waiting for me in adulthood no—you'll excuse the expression—money. My wife and I got married in the old-fashioned way. Thanks to student loans, we began our life together just like real Americans—with a negative net worth.

That was the good part of my WASP inheritance—a more or less honorable past, a clear eye, and a piece of open road stretching endlessly forward into the American future. It was all good. What there was of it, at any rate. There was one thing missing. Neither Brewster nor Winthrop nor any of those voluble preacher-men following on behind them had bequeathed to me their own faith in God. A critical omission, that. It must be in there somewhere, I've long thought, packed in alongside the memories of prep schools and happy pants and sailing regattas—not to mention my own metronomically regular attendance at Episcopal churches up and down the East Coast. It must have been in there, I thought, but I just couldn't find it. I was white, Anglo, and Saxon. That much was self-evidently plain. But was I really Protestant? Was I worshipping God according to my own lights? Was I even a non-denominational believer? Even now, it pains me to admit that I was not.

SOME KIND OF PROTESTANT

I have been wandering in the desert for so long that I'm not sure where a search for faith should begin. The possibilities seem dauntingly numerous. Should it begin with the wise men of letters—with those famously persuasive witnesses named Belloc and Chesterton and Lewis and such like? Should it begin with the brand-name leaders of institutional religion, in either their homespun or elaborately costumed iterations? Should it begin with the sacred texts of Scripture that have stood the millennial test of time? Should it begin by just looking around, with a window-shopping tour of the houses of worship currently on offer? Or, as long as I'm up and around anyway, should it begin by engaging seriously if not literally with the pamphleteers prospecting at my front door?

My undisciplined answer in recent months has been, as students of the reserved New England personality could have predicted, all of the above. I started by spreading the word 'round my personal and professional circles that, as I now intended to commence an inquiry of faith, spiritual guidance would be welcome and tales of inspiration would be especially well-received. The response has been immediate, torrential, and quite beyond my capacity to absorb. Friends and associates have been crowding in, pressing tracts into my hands, inviting me on "journeys" in bewildering variety, warning me against false prophets (whom, it appears, are swarming in ominous numbers), and pointing me in the direction of epiphanic possibility. One well-intentioned neighbor insisted that I join him on a tour of the Holy Land where I could "walk in the steps of Christ." (Whoa. Now, I'm intimidated. I'm not ready to walk in the steps of Joel Osteen.) Over these past few months, I have been the recipient of copious amounts of instruction, uplift, and prayerful concern and, for all of those good intentions, I have advanced not a single step closer to God.

But I may not be as dumb as I look. Perhaps, just perhaps, I thought, the place to begin is at the beginning. And so I think back to the last fully satisfying religious experience of my life. It had to be that day, soft and sunny, and now more than a half-century past, when I married Miss Jane in a small church in upstate New York. It was a Catholic church, and I was, accordingly, present under some duress. After extensive negotiations with the small-town priest, a genial and wily fellow who in the movie version of his life could have been played appositely by Bing Crosby, I now confess that I traded away the religious freedom of my own children. My only defense is that it seemed like a good deal at the time. Miss Jane was present and gloriously nubile, while the children were absent and wholly theoretical. Time would tell a different story, of course, as Miss Jane began to bear Catholic children with impressive regularity.

I mentioned that bit of wedding-day duress. My adoring grandmother, then still resident in the old Moody farmhouse raised in 1690, declined to attend our wedding ceremony. More to the point, she instructed me *sotto voce* not to send announcements to anybody she knew, lest word spread through northern New England that her favorite grandson was marrying a Catholic. My grandmother had taken an immediate shine to Miss Jane, and, as the daughter of outspoken abolitionists, Edna Moody Neal was a determined foe of bigotry in most of its ugly forms. But for a woman set firmly in her ways at approximately 90 years of age—in a moment of uncharacteristic vanity, she had erased all documentation of her birth and then willfully forgot the details—my wedding was simply a covered bridge too far. Even into the middle years of the 20th century, as my grandmother and her sister would recall colorfully for us young 'uns, every old Maine family nursed dark tales from the French and Indian War. These tales no doubt hardened in the telling over the years and, by the time they reached my ears, native Americans never—*never*—appeared as noble savages or as friendly neighbors or as dimwitted trading partners or even as oppressed minorities. They appeared exclusively as pillagers and scalpers and kidnappers. In some ways even worse, under the malign influence of their French masters, they appeared as Catholics. Dreaded Catholics.

It was thus bowed under the considerable weight of family baggage that I recently accompanied Miss Jane on an exploratory visit to her local church. She couldn't have been more pleased. Raised in a fervently religious family, the proud alumna of a convent school, the star lector at her parish, the most diligent student in her Bible-study

group, and the mother and grandmother of numerous con-
scripts into the legions of Rome, Miss Jane is in some re-
spects, both pastoral and doctrinal, more Catholic than the
pope. She is also the most faithful woman I know. And I
intend that term not just in the marital sense, for which I
am most grateful, but in the literal sense. She is full of
faith, so much so that when she departs this world she ex-
pects with unshakeable confidence to enter the next and
better world after no more than minimal administrative
delay. The old hymn had it right. Miss Jane is a Christian
soldier, marching onward.

Despite my high hopes, and Miss Jane's even higher
hopes, our first visit did not go well. I made a rookie mis-
take and sat 'way back in some kind of an acoustical black
hole. (The star lector sat up front with the elaborately costumed officiants.) The presiding priest was a short, dark
man who, thanks presumably to a few years of German
education, transposed his v's and w's in a particularly off-
putting manner. Given the hall's public-address problems,
compounded by the teutonic dipsy-doodle, I didn't understand a single word he said. Not one. And Miss Jane and
I didn't have much to talk about on the way home.

The following Sunday, overcompensating, I sat with
the star lector in the front row, no more than ten feet from
the priest, whom I now recognized as an African of the
sub-Saharan variety. At one point in the homily, he looked
directly into my eyes and asked imploringly, "Would you
like to renew your marital wows?" I shrugged my lack of
interest. I guess all of us who've been married a half-cen-

tury could use a few extra kilowatts in the marital bed chamber, but I wasn't looking for dating advice, thank you very much, dispensed in a singsong voice by a diminutive celibate. Miss Jane, sensing a communication unconsummated, leaned over and whispered, "He asked if you'd like to renew your marital vows." *Oh, is that it? Now, I'm offended. Why would I do that? I meant those vows the first time.* Again, there was not much to talk about on the way home.

In the established manner of New England eccentrics, a habit that has left the rest of the country uncharmed for centuries, I then began to talk to myself. The conversation went something like this. First, I reviewed the mental file labelled, "Rome." Yes, as a philosophical proposition, I have long favored the general notion of the mediating structure. But no, it would be difficult to embrace unreservedly any mediating structure that could conceive a program as morally deranged as the Inquisition. Yes, I find much to admire in the principle of subsidiarity. But no, that so-called bedrock principle seems to have been discarded too casually whenever a Crusade promised the raw satisfactions of blood and soil. Yes, I resonate approvingly to both halves of the First Amendment guarantees on the separation of church and state. But no, when Constantine converted to Christianity, the Roman state began to crush the pagan religions of most of his imperial subjects and all of his imperial predecessors. Yes, I have been much impressed with Rome's unflinching opposition to Communist ambition. But no, Rome's performance in the sex scandals of the priesthood has been unacceptable by any measure. And so it went, back and forth.

That last matter weighed heavily in the balance. I remember dining back in the Eighties with a prominent Catholic theologian. You would know his name. He seemed troubled and wanted to talk. Over a two-hour, no-martini lunch, he told me in tormenting detail about the problems with the seminaries, the problems with the urban parishes, the problems with the hierarchy itself. In his telling, homosexual predation was everywhere. I felt his pain and responded with an incisive glimpse into the obvious: "You've got to call them out. You have the platform and the credibility. These problems never solve themselves. They only get worse." My dining companion was, I thought then and continue to think today, a basically honorable man. But he found himself up against a mediating structure that is universal and apostolic and damn-near impregnable. He did not call them out. And the problems, as you may have read, did not solve themselves.

For me at least, and for now at least, all roads do not seem to lead to Rome. This much I think I know: I don't want a mediating structure getting between me and my God. I must be some kind of a Protestant.

THE VALUE OF PRAYER

I n the matter of psephological sorting, which is the bitter and inevitable residue of the mania for hardening our political categories, you can move me, at least intermittently, from the column marked "Proud American Citizen" to the column marked "Angry White Male."

I met Brett Kavanaugh back in the Nineties and then watched with swelling admiration as he made his name the hard, old-fashioned way—by pursuing high purpose with stakhanovite effort. I shook his hand once or twice, but, more to the point, I knew who he was. He had attended Yale a generation after I did, but it remained in fundamental ways the same place I had loved as an undergraduate. There were two classes of people at Yale in those years, and they were separated neither by epidermis nor genitalia as they are today. They were separated by brainjuice. There were a few geniuses and a lot of reasonably bright students who worked hard. Brett and I were in that latter group.

Two years ago, I watched the United States Senate, once described as the world's greatest deliberative body, split evenly on the question of Brett's nomination to the Supreme Court. One half of the Senators were impressed by his extraordinary achievements as student, lawyer, judge, husband, father, and citizen. The other half placed greater weight, or so they said, on wild and unsupported accusations.

On October 5, 2018, the evening before the final vote, I found myself praying. I prayed for Brett. I prayed for my country. I even prayed for the Democratic Party, which had once been described as a great political institution. I prayed that 49 Democratic Senators would not be unanimous in ignoring the evidence and presuming Brett's guilt.

My prayers were answered, I suppose you could say. Brett was confirmed and West Virginia Democrat Joe Manchin, his mind no doubt concentrated by imminent encounter with his homestate electorate, voted "aye." But the official photograph of Brett's swearing-in by Chief Justice John Roberts may have been worth a thousand prayers. Brett's wife, taut and tearful as she holds the Bible, and his two daughters, drained and grim, look as if they've stayed overlong at the funeral of a close family friend. They don't look as if their prayers have been answered.

****

As you can see, I'm new at this business. Praying, that is. With my devotional habits unformed, and the guiderails still in the packing case, I have been wildly promiscuous, spraying off prayers in all directions and on too many quotidian occasions. When I pause to think about it, of course, I understand that it is not in His nature to fire up a 24/7 Help Line for the prompt address of my every passing whim. (This praying has always been a tricky business. George Carlin, who was the last of our truly incorrect comedians, was once asked if he prayed. A famously lapsed Catholic, Carlin replied, "Sure, but not to God. I pray to Joe Pesci. He seemed like a guy who could get things done.")

My problem is that I don't pause to think about it. I now leap to prayer as a first resort. I'm the boy who can't wait to take his new bike for a spin on birthday morning. Plainly, I need some structure to this new life of prayer, some rigor that does not seem to come pre-assembled from the packing case. The last thing I want is for Him to check Caller ID—*Hmm, it's him again*—and then make Himself unavailable.

I've thus started where I've been told to start by those older and more secure in the faith—with the most dazzling and redundantly be-medaled apologists in the Christian pantheon. And as an orderly sort, I've proceeded in alphabetical rank, beginning with Belloc before moving on to Chesterton. After each essay, each tract, each book, I feel like saying to the authors, "Charmed, I'm sure." Both of them are erudite and lambent and, when you least expect it, esoterically amusing. The problem, for me at least, is that they seem to be speaking intramurally, as if they are defending Christianity from inside the fortified walls of a faith village. I'm a hard case, admittedly. I need more than rebuttal to the blaring secular voice. I need to be *moved* from where I am, which is decidedly extramural, to where they are, which from all appearance is safely at home in the grace of God.

It was with receding expectations, then, that I turned
to Clive Staples Lewis. I doubt that a year has gone by
over the past half-century when I have not been urged by
at least one friend to spend quality time with the legendary C. S. Lewis. (He would have been more legendary
still had he not died the same day an American president
was assassinated in Dallas.) I remember the day when I
was first so importuned. The friend, improbably, was
Charles W. Colson, a senior aide in the Nixon White
House who all these years later is still identified in the
press as a "Watergate conspirator." (He wasn't. He was a
conspirator in the Daniel Ellsberg case, for which he paid
in hard jail time.) Colson's brand of politics, to be candid,
made even hardened street pols look as if they were playing Nerf Ball. On a shelf overhanging the guest chair in
Colson's office, he placed a sign that epitomized his tac-
tical approach. It read: "If you've got them by the balls,
their hearts and minds will follow." This was in the Nixon
White House, mind you, which was—in terms of social
convention at least—the Pat Nixon White House.

For all of his faux-swagger, Chuck Colson may have
been the most able man I ever met, by which I mean that
he could get big things done in little time. An Ivy Lea-
guer's brain, a Marine's brawn, a zealot's passion—Colson was the ultimate bureaucratic weapon. One afternoon
in 1973, I was dining in an unfashionable Washington
restaurant with my friend John Sears, who had served as
a White House political aide in a role slightly junior to
and not infrequently competitive with Colson. As was the

custom in those days, a vendor scooted through the tables with copies of the city's great afternoon newspaper, the *Washington Star*. (It was great for, among a few other reasons, employing me for a time.) The lead story, which was splashed across the front page, reported that Chuck Colson had converted to Christianity. I arched an eyebrow and tossed the paper to Sears, who read the first few paragraphs and then said with profound professional respect, "If Colson's turned to Christ, the Devil better watch his ass." Indeed. Colson soon founded the most ambitious prison ministry in the history of Christendom.

I took it to heart, then—as more of a directive than a suggestion—when Colson, recently indicted for high crimes and felonies, sent me a note saying that Lewis's *Mere Christianity* had saved his life and was likely to save mine. (My copy is so well-thumbed that Colson may have sent me his own copy. Memory fails.) I plunged in straightaway, working my way through a volume that, frankly, I found to be a hard, uphill slog. It had no . . . rhythm. The book is, basically, a compilation of BBC radio scripts—Winston Churchill thought Lewis could bring a bit of Christian uplift to wartime Britain, which he doubtless did—and is thus written for the ear rather than the eye. One of my own occupational sins has been the writing of television scripts for more than 20 years, during which time I drained more poetry from the English language than most Literature majors have read in a lifetime. To this day, when I read a broadcast script, I am distracted by the stylistic artifice and left unmoved by either argument or rhetoric. (Now, if the good professor Lewis had done me the courtesy of reading *Mere Christianity* aloud in a perfectly modulated Oxbridge accent, perhaps my experience with it would have been more satisfying.)

In recent times, I have worked my way across the balance of the Lewis bookshelf, a formidable collection that includes, conspicuously, the Narnia stories and *The Screwtape Letters*. Not to overstate my disappointment with these almost universally beloved books, but they did nothing for me beyond the provision of pleasant diversion. Lewis writes gracefully, and powerfully, but in my own underdeveloped condition, I need more than allegorical suggestion. I need *instruction*.

Now, I don't mean to suggest that my faith inquiry has become the Bataan death march of spiritual journeys. Not at all. From the first day, from the very first page of the very first book, I have been enriched by this inquiry. My understanding of the Christian proposition has been much enlarged and much improved. But after full-immersion in the literary world of C. S. Lewis, I had almost resigned myself to a non-speaking role in the endless conversation about the mystery of faith. I had almost abandoned hope for an actual conversion to faith.

It was thus a stroke of luck, or perhaps a providential nudge, when I stumbled across a trove of Lewis's letters. It seems that I have not been alone. Many of his readers over the years have wanted to know exactly what I wanted to know—*Yes, Professor, but what does the story mean?*

How can I apply your allusive insights to my own life? How can I find Him? How should I pray to Him? And will my prayers really make any difference? In his responses to these private entreaties, Lewis, bless him, had been openly didactic.

As just one example from dozens, here is Lewis dispensing compressed wisdom on the meaning and value of prayer: "There is no question *whether* an event has happened because of your prayer. When the event you prayed for occurs, your prayer has always contributed to it. When the opposite event occurs, your prayer has never been ignored; it has been considered and refused, for your ultimate good and the good of the whole universe. (For example, because it is better for you and for everyone else in the long run that other people, including wicked ones, should exercise free will than that you should be protected from cruelty or treachery by turning the human race into automata.)"

Read that paragraph again. It tells us most of what we need to know about prayer. This man Lewis is speaking our language.

THE DECLINE AND FALL OF THE PROTESTANT SERMON

T he Episcopal Church of my youth, in a memory now fading around the edge but still vivid at the core, was a place of binary judgments. In those days now long gone, there was right and there was wrong—and never were the twain to be conflated. God's Commandments, which concretized Christian principles, were not offhandedly suggestive. They were starkly dispositive. Old-school sermons pushed home the point that there was His way and the dark way and, *pace* the triangulators, not much at all in the way of a *via media.*

When it came to moral conundra, that is to say, the intellectual living was easy. Clarity had been pressed upon us: We all knew where we stood, which was on the wrong side of the bright red line dividing saint from sinner. And we all knew what we had to do. As John F. Kennedy put it unforgettably in another context, we had to do better. (You had to be there. JFK's salty Boston accent gave eternal life to the mundane phrase.)

As even a casual student of human affairs might have guessed, we didn't do better. In the increasingly politicized view of "mainline" Protestantism, we began to do worse. And the Episcopal Church, with theatrical reluctance, seized the opportunity to gather more extra-cathedral responsibility into its own well-manicured hands.

It was toward the middle of the Sixties when I first

noticed that my church had promulgated its own foreign policy. In matters of war and peace, as also in matters of wealth and poverty, Episcopalians rolled out a series of pronouncements—in sermons, so-called—that were both rhetorically perfervid and objectively anti-American. From the exquisitely carved pulpits of what had once been houses of worship, those of us still trapped in the pews were informed that in Latin America, in Europe, in Africa, and most egregiously of all, in Southeast Asia, America's policy was, in a mendacious usage of an old and honorable word, *wrong*.

Why was America wrong? Well, take your pick, responded our triangulating pastors. America was wrong because we were disproportionately prosperous or because we were historically tainted. In the WASPiest of the WASP churches, there was even the suggestion, at first cloaked and furtive, that America was wrong because we were white. These pronouncements were not Scripturally based. They were not even thought-based. They reflected, rather, a fatal attraction to the editorial page of the *New York Times*, which for two generations had served as Holy Writ for the secular Left.

It was no more than a few years later that the Episcopal church, my church, opened a Bureau of Domestic Affairs, with an apparent mandate to accelerate change in the area of sexual mores. Reproductive rights, gay rights, gender rights, do-over rights—every glandular velleity seemed to be approved explicitly by church doctrine, at least as it came to be interpreted by the clerisy.

One chilly morning, I found myself at an Episcopal gathering in Portsmouth, New Hampshire when the presiding bishop announced that he was gay. Unlike my pew-mates, this declaration drew from me, a trained observer of the human parade, no gasps of shock and awe. (Stylistically speaking, His Eminence was not in deep cover.) You will be relieved to learn that a pack of Green Mountain boys did not then bolt down the aisle, drag the screaming prelate from his altar and, egged on by a mob of jeering ruffians, stone him to death in historic Market Square. Not at all. But you may be disappointed to hear that the congregation did not even subject him to a classic New England stare-down. No, they leapt to their feet and gave him a sustained and lusty ovation.

I remember asking myself at the time, what is it, exactly, that these people are applauding? We are in the House of God, are we not? We are not in some storefront campaign headquarters, are we? To accept our presiding bishop seemed like the Christian thing to do. To cheer him wildly seemed like an ideological thing to do.

The last time I attended an Episcopal service, I was informed—in a sermon, so-called—that it was God's Will that the minimum wage be raised to 15 dollars per hour. I had not gleaned that particular insight from my own Bible reading and I had two reactions. The first was a fervent hope that, if He finally speaks to me, we will not dribble away our precious time reviewing, bullet point by bullet point, the political agenda of, say, Charles Schumer. My second thought was that when divinity students devise

economic policy, not to mention national-security strat-
egy, they are likely to look silly, much like a cast of daft
characters escaped from a Monty Python sketch.

It goes without saying, but perhaps it needs to be re-
peated now and then, that if we as individuals wish to
gross up a worker's pay from the ten dollars of value he
produces to the 15 or 20 dollars he prefers, good for him
and good on us. Charity is a widely approved activity,
even so far as I can tell by the atavistic lights of the Episcopal Church. But to contend that raising the minimum
wage provides some general social benefit is—what's the
word we're looking for here?—*wrong*, and those who so
contend, and I say this with a heart brimming with Christian fellowship, must be reckoned either nitwits or char-
latans.

The decline and fall of the Protestant sermon triggered in me more than a sense of frustration. It triggered
a sense of loss and spurred me to a search for the real
thing—the old-time religion preached by men unclouded
by doubts about Him, and undistracted by the city lights
of contemporary politics. I won't claim that my inquiry
was deep or scholarly. It was more of an amateur spelunk-
ing in church records of the late 17th and early 18th centuries—in the years, that is, leading up to the Great
Awakening of 1739. I began with the words of my own
forebears, men named Sewall and Mather and Edwards
and Moody.

They had much in common, these Yankee preachers.
Among the best-educated men in their respective home-

towns, they had been schooled not only in history, literature, and Scripture, but in classical mythology in both its
Greek and Roman canons. Their sermons, many of them
surviving in published form, read today like spruced-up
pamphlets—bracing, evocative, hortatory. They were
crafted with literary care. There was nothing *ad libitum*
about a sermon delivered to a jam-packed and more than
occasionally snow-bound New England church. And they
were discursive, most of them, notably short on pith. (A
"feather man" patrolled the aisles, tickling awake—and
mortifying—any congregants who had nodded off.) Many
of these sermons were structured—hinged somewhere
near the middle—to allow for a midday break for lunch.
It was the Lord's Day, after all, and the faithful could
scarcely claim they had better things to do.

(Indulge, please, a fugitive thought born of full im-
mersion in well-wrought 18th-century declamation. Along
with many other Americans, I have over the course of a
lifetime been swept away by the powerful language of
Jefferson's Declaration. His ideas have engaged my mind
and secured my assent. It was his eloquence, though—the
rolling thunder of patriotic prose—that won my heart.
Today, Jefferson speaks to us across the centuries in a language only superficially similar to our own. So is it possible that those brand-new Americans of 1776, all of
whom had been steeped in high-order eloquence from the
time they could walk to church, were left unmoved by Jefferson's majestic language? Is it possible that they were
able to focus on the ideas themselves, encased in what to

them might have seemed straightforward, even unadorned presentation? Is it possible that, in the absence of patriotic trill, they could more clearly hear and thus more rationally appraise the fundamental proposition of the Declaration? I wonder. Thus endeth the apostrophe.)

As I worked my way through the ancestral trove, a few patterns began to form. Almost all of my preacher-men had delivered at one time or another an "election sermon," in which the pastor spun commentary on recent voting returns to a congregation that customarily included both the governor and the colonial legislature. (The modern reader will perhaps not be surprised to learn that God's favorite sons, in His inscrutable way, seem to have prevailed in every electoral contest.) Another staple was the "artillery sermon," which called for the preacher to address military matters of general concern and then pray over the troops. (Pastors, then as now, did not excel at military analysis.) And then there were the many fixed stars in the church calendar—anniversaries, holidays, and the like—none more resoundingly observed than January 30, which marked the execution of Charles I in 1649. Among his more conspicuous sins, Charles had married a Catholic and raised taxes. Cromwell's republicans found both actions to be inexcusable, as did much of New England, which, it would appear, was then crawling with anti-papists and proto-supplysiders. Protestant ministers danced on Charles's grave for decades until he was replaced atop the colonial Most Wanted list by George III himself.

What I found in the old-time religion is that, at least from the pulpit, there was much dreary talk of the "proper ends of civil government." The pastors, the most ambitious among them anyway, were indefatigable in their search for "just arrangements" between their flocks and the temporal powers of the day. And they took it upon themselves not only to identify but to adjudicate the proper balance between the jostling claims of citizen and state.

What I found in the old-time religion, albeit dressed up in distracting period garb, was pretty much what I'd found in contemporary religion. What I found, in a word, was politics. Seemingly high-minded, but ultimately tawdry politics.

It was at this point that rosy-fingered dawn began to creep in. What, I asked myself, if I have been looking for faith in all the wrong places? Is it possible that I've been captured by the infrastructural conceit of organized religion—namely, the presumption that God can be found only in a building designated officially by secular authority as a House of Worship? What if I have been lulled by the unexamined premise that the taller the steeple, the grander the organ, the more elaborate the candelabra . . . you know, the premise that costly man-made symbols bring us closer to God and are thus required for the enrichment and dissemination of His message?

Is that true? Has any of that ever been true? What if, just for discussion's sake, I were to invite God over to my house? And what if I were to worship Him there? And what if I were to feel His presence, and then His grace, all around me? Would mine then become a house of worship, not for purposes of tax exemption but for the purpose of saving my soul?

What if, to carry the point as far as it will go, the theatrical presentation of church services—the soaring proscenia, the blaring music, the exotic costumes—serve not to purify and enhance but rather to distort and diminish His message? Is it possible that highly organized religions, egregiously those with their catechistic market-differentiators codified at great length and in fine print, serve as a barrier first to exploration and subsequently to belief? If my own experience can be admitted as evidence, it seems very possible, indeed.

I mean no disrespect here. I am not saying that honest worship can never break out in large and tax-advantaged buildings. Miss Jane and other credible witnesses argue persuasively to the contrary. I am saying merely that those of us who seek a closer relationship with God need not confine ourselves to Sunday-morning excursions, as if we were starved parishioners craving the bespoke hamburgers available only from vendors licensed explicitly by the Burger King corporation. Churches can be wonderful institutions, community pillars. We citizens place high value upon them, and we should. But I am confident after consulting the sacred texts that God does not issue exclusive franchises, one to a neighborhood. Undocumented worshippers are neither encouraged by church authority nor acknowledged by government bureaucracy, but they are tolerated, at least for now, by both.

Back in the third century, Saint Cyprian of Carthage pronounced apodictically: *Extra ecclesiam, nulla salus. Outside the church, there is no salvation.* Cyprian had based his statement (loosely) on the Gospel of Mark, and the Roman church down through the centuries has based its dogma (occasionally) on the Carthaginian's pronouncement. I would not quarrel with Bishop Cyprian, but I would contend that, while I may have left the building, I approach closer by the day to the very heart of the church.

While we're on the subject, let's tuck a note in the time capsule. I see my evolving views as neither old-school heresy nor outer-fringe kookery. For all manner of reasons—from the managerial to the technological to the epidemiological—I suspect that history will soon record a generational surge in the kind of quiet, retail Christianity suggested here. Check back with me in 50 years or so.

THE KITCHEN DEBATES

I met Christopher Hitchens in Washington sometime in the 1980s and, almost immediately, fell in love. As a television producer, that is. I was putting out a few hundred chat shows each year and—mired as I was in the boilerplate capital of the world, where the fanny-covering language of choice was bureaucratese—I could never find enough good chatters.

There was fun-loving old John McCain, of course, who was reliably keen to possibilities for self-promotion. So keen, in fact, that he would agree to appear on a show and then, on the way to the studio, call from his car to inquire as to what topic he might be asked to address. When it came to national television exposure, Senator McCain required no foreplay. There was young Anthony Fauci of the National Institutes of Health, eager to become the public face of the fight against AIDS. For a legendarily over-scheduled professional, the good doctor seemed to be remarkably available for television hits. (In the world of broadcast journalism, the single most important ability is availability.)

There were other talking heads, Reliables both New and Old, who could be stayed by neither sleet nor snow from their appointed media rounds. (When ambitious young Beltway creatures would ask if I could make them famous, I could usually deflect them by saying that I would be happy to do so, but they would have to wait for one of the 300 people who appear on television to die.) But none was more refulgent than Christopher Hitchens, who would soon establish himself as the gold standard guest for talk-show television.

Hitchens was a glib Brit. He had not excelled in the classroom at Oxford but he had spent some time there, made well-connected friends, picked up a degree (a third, he once admitted), and then found a place for himself in the bright set of modish London. After that, it was off to America and the main chance.

Hitchens's accent was unmistakably English but not offputtingly regional, which added at least 20 points to his IQ in the ears of Anglophiliac listeners. Almost always, it seemed, he had just returned from Damascus or Pyongyang or some godforsaken place and could thus be presented more or less plausibly as a "reporter," as the man, that is, who had been there and seen it with his own eyes and, not incidentally, had secured an explosive one-on-one interview with The Man Himself, he being, not atypically, some dusty tribal chieftain or despotic head case. Hitchens could vouchsafe to our audience, or so ran the subtext of our segments with him, the secrets of a dark society closed to all but the most resourceful journalists.

Best of all, from my point of view, Hitchens was prepared to discourse on almost any subject and on indecently short notice. He did so crisply, memorably, and apparently knowledgeably. I slid in that "apparently" only because Hitchens's assertions seemed to grow in confidence as discussion ranged beyond the known world to impenetrably obscure corners of the globe. My professional views in such situations tended to be latitudinarian. If a writer has taken the trouble to airmail himself to Mogadishu, I empathized, he is entitled to present himself as an authority in all things Mogadishuan. (Not with Hitchens, but with certain others who shall be nameless, we felt obliged by experience to extend this courtesy for no more than 60 days.)

Important also to his television appeal—and this is never to be underestimated—Hitchens never bothered to conceal his contempt for most of America's economic arrangements and for all of her foreign-policy preferences. His own politics were dogmatically and revolutionarily Left—"Trot," as he and his coterie would say, referring to their deep and deeply implausible attachment to Leon Trotsky, the "good Communist" of the Bolshevik revolution. (It is a romantic trope of the hard Left that the loser in a power struggle, almost any loser, would have been much the superior leader of the revolution, almost any revolution, than the historical winner.) Hitchens's unreconstructed Leftism played well with our viewers. There is a masochistic streak snaking through semi-well-educated America that loves a good beating administered by a literate, condescending, and preferably dissolute Oxbridgian. Hitchens served that audience jolly well, and I loved him for it.

That was my relationship with Hitchens for most of a decade. Casual, correct, and thoroughly transactional. Every now and again I would offer him airtime, the inflatable cushion upon which his reputation as an "expert" floated, and in return he would give me a few minutes of well-turned and caustic commentary. Slam bam. As we used to say as he waved his goodbyes, "Domino's Pizza and Christopher Hitchens deliver."

I never knew him well. Indeed, I was never quite sure what to call him. People who knew him not at all called him Chris. That was a tell, identifying a Hitchens groupie, a member of what was then a tiny dissident cell in Reagan's rightish D.C. His friendly acquaintances called him Christopher. His good friends seemed to call him Hitch. (He sometimes called himself The Hitch, which would have been insufferably third-personist save for the hint of a redeeming twinkle.) One day, after a long shoot, I called him Hitch and he shot me a reproving glance. I retreated to the safe space. "Christopher" it would be.

I learned two other things about Hitchens during those early years, both of them so distinctive as to be almost singular. The first was his unusual relationship to strong drink. It is the convention of television producers to provide a "green room"—so-called for reasons lost to history, or at least to me—as a pre-show refuge for nervous or underprepared guests to gather themselves before impending humiliation. The producers ply the guests with soft drinks and emollient small talk, the objective being to nudge them from where they are, which is in a state of near-panic, to where you hope they will be when the camera blinks, which is in some simulacrum of a personal comfort zone. As a producer, your interests are thus aligned perfectly with your guests'. You want them to perform at their best.

From his very first appearance with us, Hitchens would have none of it. He would cast his eyes cursorily over the green room and, finding nobody worth his time, proceed to wander off. That first time, anxious that I had somehow managed to lose a guest in a mid-sized office building, I went looking for him and found him in an empty office, talking on the phone as he smoked hungrily and sipped generously from a tumbler filled with a suspiciously dark liquid. The Hitch was not nudging me toward my personal comfort zone.

I sat down across from him, determined not to let him escape my clutches yet again. In no apparent hurry, he continued to talk on the phone, filling the tumbler as needed, which needs gradually accelerated until, finally, they arose at unnervingly brief intervals. The minutes passed like hours. When he finally rang off, we were up against the clock and I escorted him directly to the set. What happened next was a real gastflabber. As the camera blinked and tape rolled, Hitchens became *more* fluent, *more* articulate, *more* riveting than he had been only moments earlier. What happened to Christopher Hitchens was what we all like to think happens to ourselves in those extra innings of an interminable cocktail party—you know, that moment when your charm becomes simply overpowering, your wit so stiletto-sharp you must take care not to nick the nice lady standing next to you. Don't try this at home, my friends, much less at the office, but I am prepared to execute an affidavit swearing to the fact that I once knew a man whose presentation skills waxed in exact correlation to his prodigious alcoholic intake.

Ah yes, the other singularity, if I may put it that way. Hitchens made it a habit, a signature conversational tic, to disparage religion in general and, more specifically, the several iterations of Christianity then most prominent in his adopted country. His tone was not contentious, his manner not table-pounding. It was as if he were remarking that the weather of late had been unseasonably humid, or that during their recent losing streak the Yankees had been playing hapless baseball. He would dispense—laconically, one after another—animadversions against preachers, popes, rituals, relics, the futility of prayer, and the manifold embarrassments of religious belief. One did not hear that sort of thing around tight-bottomed and over-lawyered Washington, D.C.

Sometime in the 1990s, we lost contact, Hitchens and I. Whether I stopped calling him or he stopped saying, "When will you need me?" I can't recall. Our relationship ended with no exclamation points expended but with schedules cluttered and interests diverged. It was my loss.

And then early in the new century, quite by chance, we fell for a season into the same social circle. Our company was a band of mid-career media types who would take off the occasional evening to gather for a round of talent-spotting, agenda-setting (yes, middle America, The Conspiracy is very much with us), and, most critically, the prying loose of marginal info-nuggets with short shelflife. (In Washington, it's not so much what you know as when you know it.) The star of these gatherings, unacknowledged by most of the ego-puffed attendees, was our man Hitchens. He would arrive, make his way around the circle, bantering as he went. (He was a world-class banterer.) Soon enough he would arrive at the kitchen, several of us in tow, and station himself next to the liquor cabinet. Once settled, he would take a stiff drink and declare himself, in no more than languid body language, open to debate. On three of these occasions, I was dumb enough to volunteer for the role of The Other Guy.

The first two debates—deeply etched in my own memory, forgotten, one hopes, by the rest of the world—took up the topic: Does God exist? With relish, and presumably anticipating a tasty forensic meal, Hitchens snatched the negative side for himself. My goodness, he was high entertainment. He drew from a vast warehouse of historical reference and literary allusion. Name any place, any newsworthy figure, and Hitchens had been there just last month, or had dined with him the previous April. Most stunning of all, Hitchens had that knack, lost now to generations of students taught by unionized teachers, of reciting poetry—not just fragments, I mean, but consecutive stanzas, full poems. I was probably not the only media type shoehorned into that young-married kitchen who was thinking, "Somebody ought to be recording this!"

Hitchens, who by that time had been debating for years, also kept handy a bag stuffed with a pro's tricks.

On those rare occasions when he was backed into a tight corner, or more likely had painted himself there, he would toss a distraction grenade at his opponent. Pausing to recall an obscure date, for instance, he would say something like, "I remember that I was no longer young. I had lost my looks and only women would go to bed with me." Or, if the argument had turned briefly on a matter of factual provenance, he would muse, "You know, I became a journalist so that I wouldn't have to rely on the news media for my information." Apostrophic flashbangs. By the time his opponent had recovered his compass, Hitchens would have scudded to higher and more defensible terrain.

His arguments against the existence of God were numerous, well-wrought, and deliciously quotable. Most of them, disappointingly, were of the faux-scientific sort, as if science might have something definitive to say about life's enduring mysteries—love, hope, faith, and the like. (It has been the habit of my lifetime to beware literary lions invoking "scientific principles" when the dialectical going gets choppy—as if they bowed to those principles in any context other than moments of rhetorical distress.)

I will not rehearse Hitchens's arguments here. You may read them for yourself in his many essays and several books on the subject. It would not spoil your own inquiry, however, if I were to inform you that his bedrock position was that religion is a superstition, clung to only by small, weak, and timid minds. He even wrote an entire book attacking Mother Teresa, then one of the two or three most-admired women in the world. Titled with Hitchensian cheek, *The Missionary Position,* the book's summary judgment was that the ascetic, fingers-to-the-bone nun was a fraud and a fanatic. I confess that I read only a chapter or two before concluding, perhaps prematurely, that Hitchens was less motivated by theological curiosity than by the potential rewards of publicity stuntery.

Well, you're wondering, how did those kitchen debates go? How did your correspondent fare? I think the word we're looking for here is "thrashed." Hitchens was the winner by unanimous decision, a judgment supported even by my own traitorous corner men, two friends for whom I had wangled invitations to the soiree. I would have felt worse about the twin beatdowns, of course, had Hitchens not thrashed Tony Blair, William F. Buckley Jr., Germaine Greer, and every other master and mistress of the public platform.

You heard it said in those days that Hitchens was the greatest living essayist in the English language. I don't know about that. I was a Joe Epstein man myself. But the greatest living debater in the English language? On that question I was, unreservedly, a Christopher Hitchens man.*

The good news, such as it was, involved post-operative effects. I had absorbed the best shots from the

---

* I mentioned a third debate with Hitchens. It must have occurred in the waning days of 2002 or the early days of 2003. The subject was the upcoming invasion of Iraq, and Hitchens astonished both me and the kitchen cabinet by declaring his unhedged support for George W. Bush's "discretionary" war. The Hitch! The *(cont.)*

toughest hombre in town, but there I was, wobbly but un-
bowed. More than that, in succeeding weeks I found myself hardened not weakened—*structurally reinforced*—in
my own burgeoning views. The ferocity of Hitchens's at-
tacks had forced me to read and to think and to pray. In
hindsight, there can be no doubt that Christopher
Hitchens, of all the unlikely people, had pushed me closer
to God. For that I am grateful to him. No, I should go
max-cliché and state that I am eternally grateful to him.

A few years later, 2010 I think it was, word raced
around the media circuit that Hitchens had been struck
with a particularly nasty disease. Throat cancer. Denizens
of the Internet's nether regions pounced on the news. It
was condign punishment, they raged, for a man who had
given voice to so much blasphemy. God was taking His
revenge, and so on. This web chatter was more than rou-
tinely despicable stuff, and I hoped that none of it would
reach Christopher. At the same time, my attention was
alerted. It is said with some conviction that there are no
atheists in foxholes. I couldn't help but wonder if the
same condition obtained in the intensive-care wards of
Houston hospitals.

---

man who could detect stains of American imperialism invisible
even to microbiologists! The man who could be heard well into
the 1980s cooing about the unappreciated virtues of Rosa Luxem-
burg! What prompted Hitchens's midnight ride from far to my left
to far to my right I will never know, but there he was, pounding
the drums of war in perfect syncopation with the neoimperialists.
Now that I think of it, I may have won that last debate. Hitchens's
anti-war friends might have sided with me.

Christopher endured a long ordeal with his implacable disease. Against all form, he did as he was told and submitted to confining regimens and gruesome treatments. Throughout, he remained chin up, once describing as "futuristic" a gizmo that shot protons through his body at hypersonic speed. Observers less directly involved might have called that same gizmo "medieval." Hitchens being Hitchens, he got a book out of it, too. If you can handle a good cry, try *Mortality,* published in 2012.

For the last year of his life, Christopher was by all accounts, including his own, a model patient even as the reality dawned that he was a doomed cancer victim. And never once did he wave the white flag. It can be recorded authoritatively that there was at least one atheist in the cancer foxhole at MD Anderson.

R.I.P., Christopher. I admired your courage, both physical and intellectual, but I very much hope that, while you won the debate, you lost the argument. Let me know, will you?

THE ROAD TAKEN

I should confess that, along the path of this journey, I once sidled up to the window prepared to bet the ranch on Mr. Pascal's proposition. A seductive fellow, Mr. Pascal.

A 17th-century intellectual so public that over the next 400 years nobody ever felt obliged to ask—"I'm sorry, to which Mr. Pascal do you refer?"—Blaise Pascal is frequently described as a philosopher and mathematician. In his posthumously published work, *Pensees,* which is still read and wrestled with to this day, he posed a question that has long teased the spiritually tentative. It went like this. Pascal posited that every human being must confront a basic question in life: Should he assume that God exists? Or should he assume that God does not exist? Simple enough, eh? If the individual opts for the former, he must deny himself some temporal pleasures of earthly passage, but, if the assumption proves to be correct, he wins personal salvation and eternal life. If he opts for the second assumption, however, he may feast on the delicacies of the human banquet, sensual and otherwise, but knows for a certainty that he will be allotted not one single day beyond physical death.

As you can see, Blaise Pascal was, at least in this instance, more of a mathematician than a philosopher. He was making it comfortable for the skeptical to occupy common ground with the faithful. If you took his wager,

you were under no obligation to believe in God. Under
the terms of his pragmatic calculation, you could merely
assume the existence of God. You could be acceptably
Christian, that is to say, without necessarily believing in
the divinity of Christ. If this strikes you as some kind of
flimflammery, well, that would be your own smallminded
judgment, not mine.

As I say, I was relieved to know that I could take Pascal's wager and declare a victory of sorts. I wouldn't be
returning from this inquiry with utterly empty hands.
Even so, I was aware that taking his bet would never be
comprehensively satisfying. It would soon reveal itself as
a philosophical cop-out, just as it had done for all those
Pascalian odds-players down through the centuries.

I then felt the urge to move on from Mr. Pascal and
was pleased to discover that I had built some momentum.
I was still spiritually malnourished, but I sensed that faith
was out there somewhere, hovering, and that my job was
not to await an epiphanic event—some version of the
Pauline conversion—but rather to open myself to the
power of The Word. My job was to let Him into *my* life,
rather than trying to barge into His.

I picked up a Bible given to me in the middle of the
last century by Grandmother Freeman. I should report that
it is in embarrassingly pristine condition. In a single sit-
ting, and relishing every verse for its King James diction,
I read the four Gospels. *(Biblical scholar alert! Avert your
eyes from what follows. We have disturbing reports of an
amateur thrashing about on your turf.)* John, who seems

to be the heartthrob of doctoral students with his propensity for complexity-verging-on-opacity, did not do it for me. William Blake may have been thinking about John when he wrote: "Both read the Bible day and night, but thou read black where I read white." I have nothing against John, personally or pastorally, but I have only one lifetime to spend on this project. Nor did Mark or Luke make the tumblers fall into place on my particular combination lock. Both of them are duly chiliastic, but they tend to veer off into clubhouse chatter in what amounts to their own Members Only lounge. (My apologies for the compounding metaphors. I'm getting there, I swear.) I have been elevated from the waiting list, praise the Lord, but I'm still no more than a provisional member of His club.

But Matthew! The much underrated Matthew! To my untrained eye, he must be reckoned either a) the apostle with prophetic powers equal to even the God whose earthly life he chronicles or b) the world's most reliable stenographer. The latter seems far more likely, with Matthew cast as the wire-service reporter who, after swearing off color and hype, locks in the timeline and then nails the quotes. Take the sermon of all sermons, which launches in Chapter 5. Matthew records the Beatitudes with what appears to be absolute fidelity to *somebody's* original text. We not only have the perfectly sculpted "Blessed are the poor in spirit for theirs is the kingdom of heaven" and "Blessed are the meek for they shall inherit the earth," but we have the soaring, "Blessed are the pure in heart for they shall see God." Ask yourself. Did Matthew jot down rough notes at deadline, making up stuff like a cable-news guy with five minutes to air? Did Matthew get a sketchy translation from some descendant of a shepherd who claimed to have wandered by the Mount that day? Or did Matthew transcribe faithfully the timeless Word of God in all its shimmering beauty?

Matthew is nothing if not comprehensive. He gets around to the Beatitudes only after he has recorded the baptism, the fast in the desert, the temptation by Satan, and even after Christ has chosen the Twelve Apostles. Every stern condemnation, every ferric commandment seems to be inscribed here. And then there is the Sermon itself, the longest speech by Jesus in the New Testament. In Chapter 6, I found myself falling into step with the familiar rhythms of the Lord's Prayer. And along the way I received a gift of insight. I now understand, finally, what people mean when they speak of the "comfort" of prayer. It is an anxiety dispersant. It is a peace finder. I even managed to forgive myself my trespasses without tripping over the sibilants.

Yes, I recited His Prayer aloud, but only after first closing my office door. There is nothing more disconcerting to our cultural overlords than public displays of religious devotion. In more than a few urban fiefdoms, peeing in the street may be frowned upon but praying in the street is cause for general alarm. (Even closed-door praying is not without its own risks. I was speaking only to God today, but I must contend with the possibility, re-

port the media, that Alexa was listening in and may have
since reported me to Mr. Bezos, or whomever is in charge
of monetizing my confessional data.)

I do not know much about Matthew. I read somewhere that in a previous life he had served as a tax col-
lector, for which I have found it in my heart to forgive
him. Whatever the details of his resume, I am indebted to
him for providing what moved me as an indispensable
vade mecum. How far has he brought me? Where are we
now? And have we encountered any disappointments
along the way?

About that last question first, yes, two disappointments.

I had hoped for many years to feel a tug, a real sleeve-
pull, toward Rome. Many of the people I cherish most in
my life are Catholics, either born to the Faith or converted
somewhere along the way. (One of the most blessed chap-
ters of a long life is that magical decade during which you
are invited to attend more mid-life baptisms than funerals.
I extrapolate no broad social trend here, but most of those
conversions within my own circle have been to Catholicism.) I long to be with them, my Catholic friends, but as
I acknowledged earlier, it is not yet to be.

The other disappointment is that as I stumbled my
way forward, advancing doggedly if uncertainly, I encountered no theatrical markers. None whatsoever. Now,
I'm not so high maintenance as to require an angelic vis-
itation backed by heavenly chorus, but a somewhat bigger
finish, I thought, would not have been out of place. These

were, from my perspective at least, developments of earth-shivering import. I have calmed myself in this matter with a memory of Malcolm Muggeridge, that dear man (who had inadvertently set off poor Hitchens by producing a hagiographic BBC documentary on Mother Teresa). Malcolm had spent years, decades, developing his own faith, and when I asked him how it had finally come together for him, he admitted that he had at one time expected a bit of punctuation—a thunderclap, perhaps, or at the least a burst of well-sung song. In the event, he said, his faith had simply "unfolded."

I am well along in my own journey—thanks to Malcolm, I see it as less of a meandering and more of an unfolding—and it is beginning to feel very much like the path toward home.

Walker Percy, one of America's great faith seekers, who posed for years as a novelist, wrote something that sticks with me. In *The Moviegoer*, Percy's protagonist, Binx Bolling, freeze-frames his own spiritual journey this way: The search is "what anyone would undertake if he were not sunk in the everydayness of his own life. To become aware of the possibility of the search is to be on to something. Not to be on to something is to be in despair."

Just so, Binx. Like you, I am on to something.

ALMOST HOME

Down through the years, Christianity has been an irresistible target for, among others, the affronted, the rapacious, the insecure, the aggrieved, the ignorant, the vicious, and the intimidated. From Pontius Pilate 2,000 years ago to Christopher Hitchens just a moment ago, some of the smartest and most powerful people in world history have devoted considerable energies to destroying the Christian religion. Some of those critics trashed the idea itself, the belief system. The worst among them, arguably, have attacked the institution, damning it and banning it, starving it and disfiguring it, burning its sacred books and exterminating its true believers.

During that long stretch, of course, other human institutions have experienced their own troubles. Political parties? They have come and gone at high speed. One of the oldest parties in the world, known to journalists of a certain age as the Grand Old Party, has yet to reach its 200th birthday. Nation states? Look at a map from a few centuries ago. It bears little similarity to your contemporary edition. Powerful families? They rotate every third generation or so, slipping inexorably from the penthouse to the windowless basement and then, once in a blue moon, reversing themselves.

Well, how about empires, those continent-spanning, citizen-bending enterprises of lore and legend? The Romans? Gone. The Ottomans? Gone. The Persians? The Spaniards? The Japanese? The Austro-Hungarians? All gone. What about the Soviets? Now, there was an empire, stretching not only from sea to shining sea, but leaping entire oceans in a vainglorious attempt to sate insatiable appetites. You had to be there to believe it, but the Soviet enterprise ended with an entirely bang-less whimper.

Well, then, what of the British empire? You remember, the one upon which the sun never set? The one celebrated so memorably in song and verse? As I write these words, the British empire, mortified by history, is struggling to hold together a tiny island nation bobbing off the northwestern coast of the European continent.

Remarkable, isn't it? While other human institutions, many of them dominant in their time, have withered and died, Christianity—the idea of Jesus Christ as the risen Lord—has grown and prospered over the very long haul of two millennia. Almost one in every three human beings alive today professes his or her faith in Jesus.

These data do not make a closing case for Christian faith, but they are highly *suggestive*: There is something extraordinarily durable in the Christian idea. For those of you poised at the starting line of a lifelong journey, you can be sure that, in accepting Christ, you are not joining some bizarre cult. You are not catching a soon-passing fad. You are joining a throng of people, a virtual human wave, all of them confident that they have already found what you have begun to look for. These data *do* make the point that, as a reasonable person reviewing the record, you would be wise at the outset of your journey to suspend your disbelief.

Now, let's take a step further. The most deadly critics of any institution are not those who criticize it or attack it, or even those who persecute its adherents. The most devastating critics are those who ridicule it. Those who laugh at it. Humor works with shreds of truth; it messes with the subconscious; it fires off unguided emotional missiles. Within totalitarian regimes, or their civilian equivalents in woke communities, humor can be powerful stuff, a dangerous and combustible substance. I, your humble correspondent, can report that I knew *exactly* when the Soviet Union was about to collapse. I was meeting in Washington with an official from the Soviet embassy—which meeting itself strongly suggested that the official was KGB—when he told me a joke about the Soviet economy. It was not a particularly good joke, something about the Soviets' (largely imaginary) GDP, but it was a joke against the regime. For the inquiring mind and, even more so for the independent spirit, jokes against the regime are improvised explosive devices. *Boom!*

A while back, I mentioned George Carlin, the stand-up comedian. He made a good living for a few decades badmouthing Christianity. Real people—whole auditoria full of them—would pay real money to hear his bare-stage, blasphemous rants. In my view, he earned those fees. He got off some good, tart lines. They lose something when printed as frozen words on a flat page—Carlin was a fine performer with a richly histrionic voice and a pair of dancing eyebrows—but it's hard to forget his acid-tipped thrusts, these among them:

- Here's Carlin taking exception to one of the Ten Commandments:
    "Coveting your neighbor's goods is what keeps the economy going."
- And here's Carlin reviewing God's job performance:
    "Something is wrong here. War, disease, death, destruction, hunger, filth, poverty, torture, crime, corruption, and the Ice Capades. . . . If this is the best God can do, I'm not impressed. This is the kind of performance you'd expect from an office temp with a bad attitude."
- And here's Carlin on the Bible's place in our public life:
    The good book is "America's favorite theatrical prop."

Ouch.

But if you ask a Carlin fan for his favorite riff, he'll remember the one about the Invisible Man, which in Carlin-speak denotes the Supreme Being. Carlin's long take ends this way: The Invisible Man "loves you . . . and he needs money. He always needs money. He's all-powerful but he can't handle money." *Badabing.*

I'm guessing—okay, I'm hoping—that by this time

you can handle this kind of verbal shot. You can absorb it, turn it over in your mind, and then react in a human way. By laughing. After which, and only after which, you can parse the joke and note that Carlin hasn't laid a glove on the Invisible Man. The people who need the money, the people who can't handle the money, are not God or even God-like creatures. They are His self-appointed agents, men and women as deeply flawed as—to pick two random examples—you and I.

If you've passed the George Carlin test, congratulations! You can now laugh at yourself, as also at your most cherished beliefs. A Christian in any time—but especially in our own censorious moment—must be flexible, loose in the joints. You may now be qualified to sit for the final exam: The Evelyn Waugh test.

The wickedly clever English novelist was known by his numerous friends and even more numerous foes to be a rebarbative personality. That's right. If you read three articles about Waugh, any three, you will come across that odd word three times. It means "repellent," but it comes with a special sauce. It seems that Evelyn Waugh, on the testimony of all who knew him, could be really, really repellent.

In his middle years, and much to the dismay of fancypants London—*secular* London—Evelyn Waugh converted loudly to Catholicism. He was now a godly man, committed fully to his new faith. Some observers were quick (and gleeful) to note, however, that the famously rebarbative personality had not been replaced immediately by a warm and anodyne successor. Waugh remained, at least for a time, obdurately Waugh-like.

One day a lady of high-church sensibilities was heard to ask the begged question, "Mr. Waugh, how can you behave as you do, and still call yourself a Christian?" Waugh replied, "Madam, were it not for my religion, I would scarcely be a human being." Exactly. Compacted in that single sentence is much of the wisdom, including the self-wisdom, that you will need to propel your own journey. Who but the Holy Spirit could have levitated the miserable Evelyn Waugh from rebarbative to marginally tolerable? (There have been quarantine days, I have no doubt, when Miss Jane prayed that He might do the same for me.)

I close with a wisp of the mighty Pascal. Faith is always and everywhere an affair of the heart. But faith rarely settles in without assent from the head. The mind turns and the heart leaps, in one sequence or the other. So you may on that account wish to begin your inquiry with the cool calculation that, in seeking God, you have nothing to lose and everything to gain. I considered that wager myself and you are welcome to it. As further precaution against early-onset spiritual fatigue, you should feel free to invoke the mighty Carlin's undervalued Eleventh Commandment, "Thou shalt keep thy religion to thyself."

To any reader who has persevered to this final page, I say, thank you. Your patience is much appreciated. But I must tell you that it's later than you think. It's well past time for you to take your own first step. And what better time than today? Go ahead—take that singular, tentative, prayerful, clumsy, glorious step now.

I send you on your way with the prayer, plucked from an old Spanish hymn, that launches my own mornings.

> *Open my eyes, Lord*
> *Help me to see your face.*
> *Open my eyes, Lord*
> *Help me to see.*
>
> *Open my ears, Lord*
> *Help me to hear your voice.*
> *Open my ears, Lord*
> *Help me to hear.*
>
> *Open my heart, Lord*
> *Help me to love like you.*
> *Open my heart, Lord*
> *Help me to love.*